HowExpert Presen  I0005357

How To Do Online Dating For Women

Your Step By Step Guide To Online Dating For Women

HowExpert with Amma Ampofo

Copyright HowExpert™
www.HowExpert.com

For more tips related to this topic, visit
HowExpert.com/onlinedatingwomen.

Recommended Resources

- HowExpert.com – Quick 'How To' Guides on All Topics from A to Z by Everyday Experts.
- HowExpert.com/free – Free HowExpert Email Newsletter.
- HowExpert.com/books – HowExpert Books
- HowExpert.com/courses – HowExpert Courses
- HowExpert.com/clothing – HowExpert Clothing
- HowExpert.com/membership – HowExpert Membership Site
- HowExpert.com/affiliates – HowExpert Affiliate Program
- HowExpert.com/writers – Write About Your #1 Passion/Knowledge/Expertise & Become a HowExpert Author.
- HowExpert.com/resources – Additional HowExpert Recommended Resources
- YouTube.com/HowExpert – Subscribe to HowExpert YouTube.
- Instagram.com/HowExpert – Follow HowExpert on Instagram.
- Facebook.com/HowExpert – Follow HowExpert on Facebook.

From the Publisher

Dear HowExpert reader,

HowExpert publishes quick 'how to' guides on all topics from A to Z by everyday experts.

At HowExpert, our mission is to discover, empower, and maximize talents of everyday people to ultimately make a positive impact in the world for all topics from A to Z...one everyday expert at a time!

All of our HowExpert guides are written by everyday people just like you and me who have a passion, knowledge, and expertise for a specific topic.

We take great pride in selecting everyday experts who have a passion, great writing skills, and knowledge about a topic that they love to be able to teach you about the topic you are also passionate about and eager to learn about.

We hope you get a lot of value from our HowExpert guides and it can make a positive impact in your life in some kind of way. All of our readers including you altogether help us continue living our mission of making a positive impact in the world for all spheres of influences from A to Z.

If you enjoyed one of our HowExpert guides, then please take a moment to send us your feedback from wherever you got this book.

Thank you and we wish you all the best in all aspects of life.

Sincerely,

BJ Min
Founder & Publisher of HowExpert
HowExpert.com

PS...If you are also interested in becoming a HowExpert author, then please visit our website at HowExpert.com/writers. Thank you & again, all the best!

Table of Contents

Introduction

I love online dating.

I can say that honestly and without reservation. Sure, there have been times when I wanted to throw my computer right out of the window, and hurl frustrated insults from my seven-story walkup, but that happens pretty frequently in "regular" dating too—except on those occasions it's usually a wine glass instead of a laptop. It's the name of the game for a woman who's looking for love in all the most adventurous and plentiful ways she can! You take the good and you take the bad and if you have just the right positive outlook, it's mostly good. That said, I'm an old pro when it comes to online dating.

I know what you're used to. You're used to being introduced to your latest boyfriend by your best friend's boyfriend. Or you're used to meeting him at a bar, or at someone's wedding after you've had a few cocktails. But if you're a vivacious woman who likes to keep her options open, you need to take your dating scene to the worldwide web. You know they don't call it by that name for any old reason; the beauty of online dating is that you have a literal world of opportunity to find new romance, a hook up, or just a really great story.

I've been on all kinds of dates, from tame dinners and drinks, to more exciting museum visits, roof-top parties or karaoke jaunts with a slew of complete strangers. I've been on dates that bored me to tears and ones that made me have to sit on my hands before rushing to text back someone I was just that excited about. On a few occasions, I've known from the moment I've met someone that we'd have absolutely NO romantic or sexual chemistry, but I've been a good sport about it and completed a date if it wasn't terrible. I've also been very pleasantly surprised by an absolutely great date that I was completely ambivalent about even *before* meeting up.

The great thing about dating is that it will never go out of style! With all the other conveniences the internet has given us, it makes perfect sense that it would impact our love lives as well. We can get just about anything we want online, so why not a date? Online dating is extremely common in our current society. It's given anyone with a laptop the ability to contact one another and communicate in the hopes of achieving sex, romance or both. It is fast, and in today's social climate, instant gratification is valued above all else. Instant messages have taken years off of intimate communications. We are Generation Now: we all want it as fast and as comfortably as we can get it.

As a woman, online dating allows you to put yourself and your most important information on display, with the opportunity to reach out to countless numbers of eligible men. Additionally, one of the greatest advantages to starting out online is learning a lot about a man before you even meet him in person, allowing you the upper hand and giving you the opportunity to gracefully evade unwanted advances if you realize you're incompatible. This proves to be a huge timesaver, and it will make your search that much more efficient. I've done the work for you, so just sit back and enjoy.

When you think about it, there are many services to choose from, and so many venues for contacting these eligible guys: email, chat rooms, instant messengers, video messaging, up to exchanging mobile numbers. But of course, there are many things you should know—rules, really—about online dating before you dive right in:

- **You'll have the pick of the litter, so to speak.**

  As I've mentioned there are so many different kinds of people, thousands of minutely different personalities, and interests. Once you create a guideline of your interests and what you are looking for in a man, simply weed through them!

- **It offers discretion.**

  No one in your day-to-day life has to know exactly what you're doing, or the details of your online pursuits, unless you want them to (and eventually you will—trust me). This can be especially helpful if at first you are apprehensive about logging on in the first place (which you have no reason to be.—be fearless!)

- **You will need to become efficient in gauging compatibility very quickly.**

  You don't want to waste days, or even weeks of your time trying to figure out if a guy is right for you. Construct a list of qualities you desire in a man and use it to avoid dead-end dates you don't truly want. You will need to make sure you are not hyper-specific with this list, otherwise it will become your downfall as you become too picky and narrow-minded in your selection process. This will hold you back from achieving the most optimal of dates. More on this later.

- **Online dating makes it very clear that you are meeting people with the direct intention of love and mating.**

  This aspect is helpful in that it removes the ambiguity from the equation. Which is what so many women end up falling victim to. How many times have you thrown your affection at a man you met in your day to day life/through friends, only to be given the innocent "I had no idea we were more than friendly" excuse? The worst.

  So long as people are interested in one another for mating purposes, the excitement of going on dates will live long and prosper. Experiencing the dating scene is also a great supplement to the personality of someone who is comfortable in their skin and interested in expanding their social prowess. If you are career oriented, you'll find a great deal of useful information within Online Dating for Women on how to enrich that aspect of your life.

Once you're done with this handy how-to guide, you'll have amazing hints on how to:

1. Add the online advantage to your day-to-day regular dating life.

We go on regular dates all the time, but imagine if you suddenly added thousands of men to your options for potential dates? Online dating will give you tons of leverage in finding the kinds of relationships you want, in an active and timely fashion. I literally wouldn't have gone on half of the dates that I've been on were it not for putting my online dating profile to good use! There are even sites where you can check out someone's profile, decide to meet up, pick a location for a date and get face to face all within the same day! If that isn't efficient, then I don't know what is.

2. Get plentiful messages from the men you really want to hear from.

When you create a truly enticing and well put together profile, you will receive plenty of messages from eligible bachelors, no matter your age, race, or whether you're drop dead gorgeous. I know what men are looking for, and it's not going to be a world class supermodel. It's going to be a great girl with a sense of humor and a confidence about her. With the information in this how-to guide, you'll be able to refine the utmost level of confidence and that, above all, will drive men to you and your profile. So prepare to attract the guys you're actually looking to meet!

3. Save the most money by making the most of free online dating sites.

I've been on pay sites, free sites, beta tested sites and iPhone apps galore. The biggest thing I've learned? You don't necessarily have to pay to play. Unless you are searching for something (or some man) with highly specific, nuanced criteria, you'll be fine using a free online dating site in your search for a great relationship. Online dating sites and services have been around for at least a decade now and have grown so popular that you don't have to sit around believing that only the poorest of losers are utilizing the free ones. So save that money for a great haircut or a new outfit to wear out on your wonderfully priceless date.

4. Create a profile that is genuine and still alluring.

You one hundred and ten percent don't have to lie, even a little bit, about yourself on your online dating profile. Using the techniques in this how-to, you can accentuate and express the greatest parts of you without having to worry about how it will come across. Everyone is looking for someone passionate about something and interested in something, and we will be improving your understanding of not only what makes you unique and pulls you out of bed in the morning, but your understanding of what you hope to gain and what kind of beau you are looking to meet!

5. Use your profile pictures to put your best face forward!

Your greatest confidence booster will be the point during which you find your "best face." That means, taking flattering pictures of yourself for sure, but also ones that are true representations of what you look like so that you don't feel as though you are putting on a front or being duplicitous with any of the men you may meet along the way. Using these tools, you'll stand out in a sea of profiles and men will get to know more about you, since we all know a picture says a thousand words. Not to mention, you'll have some great images to pull from for any occasion.

6. Sharpen your interpersonal and social skills while hunting down Mr. Right.

Strengthening your ability to communicate will do some very awesome things not only for your dating future, but for your interactions outside of online dating. As straightforward as you can teach yourself to be, the better. You'll be meeting so many new people that you'll be forced to be incredibly interactive, which only works to your benefit, since interpersonal skills are super important for anyone to have. If you're on the shy side, all the better; if you're way more outgoing, there's a great opportunity to extend your social circle with dates who are actually awesome men but who just lack chemistry with you.

7. Make every weekend (and even weeknights!) truly memorable and fun-filled.

If you've ever been bored to tears on a Thursday night, or your cable television primetime lineup is on temporary hiatus...you've just found a great excuse to get out of the house! I love reading a book or just relaxing after work just as much as the next person, but if you're looking to spice things up or utilize your free time a little bit more, this is the way to do it. Now, when people ask you how your weekend was, you'll be more likely to tell them something a little more interesting than "oh, you know, I stayed in with the cat."

8. Inspire confidence in yourself and feel great about the adventurous woman you know you can be.

This will be the most important of every single thing this book has to offer. Because online dating opens up a slew of new opportunities for romance and hook ups, you'll grow confidence and also have a more positive outlook on the dating scene. The more dates you go on, the less likely you'll be to fall back on the comfort of apprehension or avoidance when it comes to other new opportunities, whether it be an arduous life challenge or something particularly ambitious that you want to do within your career. As a heterosexual woman, going on countless dates made me fearless in the face of much of my opposition.

9. Be the envy of all your girlfriends with your new found dating prowess!!!

Online dating is so popular now that the majority of my girlfriends (and my guy friends) use it. And we all keep very busy; we love sharing tips and tricks as well as horror stories. Being a veteran of the technology makes me somewhat of a mentor and an advice queen amongst my crew. Dating can be difficult for us women in general and when you add the aspect of making it happen online, all kinds of interesting obstacles and questions can crop up. You'll need to be adequately prepared. So with that said, follow me on this journey to handing over the greatest online dating arsenal: allow me to help you be your best dating asset!

Chapter 1: Your Level of Effort

How much time would you say you have to devote to the search for love? Weeks? A day or two? Just a few passing moments?

No matter if your goal is just to dabble in it or to completely immerse yourself, your best bet is to figure this out as soon as possible. Gauging your level of interest will play a very large role in how others view your profile. When you don't put much effort into what you throw into your online dating profile, or if you leave it too short, it may look as though you just took care of it in passing. Nothing about that is particularly as alluring to the opposite sex. Sure, people—and especially some guys—may not be as interested in what you write as much as how you look (I'm just being honest, as theory dictates that men are more visual creatures than women!). But that is no excuse to go forward with a poorly done or half completed profile.

If you're not willing to immerse yourself fully in the hunt for a great man, you'll notice that you won't be anywhere near successful in securing any awesome prospects. Just like everything else in this life, you have to be willing to put in the work to be rewarded with the benefits. This isn't to say that you need to spend every waking moment with your online dating profile search, but it helps to be aware of how much energy you're expending in relation to how many responses, and finally how many dates you get through the site. And you should never forget that practice makes perfect.

FIGURE OUT HOW MUCH TIME YOU WANT TO DEVOTE TO THE SEARCH.

If I've said it once, I've said it a million times: it's fine if you want to spend mere minutes on the online dating circuit, or if you decide to become really engrossed in it and devote hours at a time. This will all depend on your interest level. But unless you have model good looks and the track-record of a five-time Oscar winning actress (which, sadly I must say that most of us do not), don't be surprised if after spending only a few minutes on your profile, you never hear from the cream of the crop kind of guy that you've initially set your sights after.

DESIGNATE A CERTAIN AMOUNT OF TIME EACH DAY (OR WEEK) TO LOOKING AT PROFILES.

One of the most important parts of this process is going to be sitting in front of your laptop (or on your Smartphone if you're an on-the-go kind of gal) and looking at profiles to get a feel of what awaits you out there. Not only do you want to learn where your options lie, but it is great to get an idea of how much you can accomplish in however long a time period you decide to spend on your search. How discerning can you be in a short span of time regarding a particular guy's profile? The search shouldn't consume your entire life, but if you want to get the most out of it all, you'll want to be poking around the website on a fairly regular basis.

If you're still skeptical, here are a few pretty awesome incentives!

Make use of Smartphone online dating apps! They were probably one of the best things that ever happened to me in online dating. In fact, every time a site that I used developed an application, I was doubly grateful. As I mentioned, I am totally a girl on the go, and finding small gaps of time in which to search definitely made a striking difference in the amount of dates I went on. Had I waited until I got home from work or whatever external activities I'd been up to, I'd most likely have been too tired to look anyone up.

You get to know that feeling you feel when you meet a guy and he's even better looking in person than he appears in his profile pictures! I promise you that there's almost nothing better than that. Actually, the feeling you get when you meet up with a guy in general for the first time and he's just exactly what you like, is phenomenal. You get to relish that over and over if you play your cards right! And either way, there's an amazing rush from hanging out waiting to see someone you've never met. It's like a blind date where you don't have the mutual friend involvement; it's really kind of exhilarating.

If you're lucky, you get taken out on some great dates and the guy will foot the bill. Teetotalers and ultra-feminists aside, if you're a girl who likes her drink, it's an awesome thing to get to evade ridiculous drink prices in the name of tradition. So not only are you learning how to save on dating site fees, but also scoring a few bucks saved here and there when you actually go out to meet up with a potential match. Keep in mind: the best way to return the favor is by being a courteous, interesting, and well put together date.

Chapter 2: Is it Just for Sex or for Romance?

Are you interested in simply going out on awesome dates or does your expectation involve finding more romance and love in a long-term setting? Be sure to approach this question from an extremely truthful standpoint! The worst thing you can do is lie to yourself or your prospective partner about your expectations. If you just want a hook up, never lead a guy on who's looking for more. Even more importantly, if you're looking for more than just one night or a few casual encounters, never allow a man to think that you're interested in being casual in the hopes that he'll change his mind about the situation.

You simply <u>cannot</u> change people at the drop of a hat and you'll be sorely disappointed if your romantic adventure doesn't turn out just how you would have hoped, I assure you. Both parties need to be crystal clear about what they hope to gain from the relationship they create once meeting offline. Truly, this is one of the biggest obstacles in coupling and it can be solved by just a few honest conversations, if not one. This is why communication is key and it is also one of the first steps to strengthening your own grasp on a high level of it.

EVALUATE YOUR ROMANTIC LEANINGS.

Stop a moment: think long and think hard about what you're looking for. In my experience, when I first started online dating, I'd only had one semi-long term relationship. I had a lot of shorter term more casual ones or just a few dates here and there, so I was completely open to whatever happened. Really, my main goal was to meet interesting, funny men as well as do some social networking. I was fresh out of college and unemployed with a lot of time on my hands so that helped immensely. As a woman who knows what she wants and is willing to dive in and explore for it, I became somewhat of a serial dater, but only because I knew better than to settle for anything less than what I thought I was worth.

*Something **IMPORTANT** to consider during this process:*

- <u>Have you just gotten out of a relationship?</u>

If you have, you need to know when you're rebounding. For the uninitiated, rebounding refers to the time period of emotional limbo that occurs at the end of a romantic or sexual relationship and before the start of a newer, healthier one. A rebound can be helpful in that transitional period between relationships. If you're feeling vulnerable after just having broken up with a boyfriend, be aware of the fact that you may just want to hook-up with someone to alleviate loneliness, or just plain horniness. BEWARE, however, of a dependency on being in a relationship; that compulsion and inability to be alone for extended periods of time can stem from more serious, unresolved issues regarding self esteem and should be completely worked out before bringing a secondary party into the equation.

DECIDE IF YOU WANT THE CASUAL RELATIONSHIP.

This relationship will be the fun, carefree and just looking to have a good, flirty, sexual experience. This is not to say that you cannot maintain these sentiments within a romantic relationship! However, the duration and the level of effort will probably be very different. Don't expect a guy to call you every single day, or constantly ask you to hang out. Additionally, you should 150% not be alarmed, jealous or saddened if it is made clear that this guy is seeing someone else while he's seeing you. Exclusivity between the two of you is not typically required and it is extremely rare.

Bear this in mind as you look for a potential mate, sexual or otherwise: many people use online dating not unlike an adult classifieds section—only it's way less sleazy and also significantly less dangerous than meeting someone blindly (disclaimer: this does not mean you have license to not be cautious at all times!). It can be liberating and helpful since it removes the awkwardness of going right up to someone and asking them to have sex with you. There are cues, some more subtle and some with a more overt execution that a person who is seeking out casual sex will utilize, body language and being overly flirtatious included.

DECIDE IF YOU WANT THE ROMANTIC RELATIONSHIP.

This relationship has a much stronger element of emotional attachment and investment, in the hope that it will lead to love and a long-term, fulfilling union for those who are involved. We are all human of course and everyone has sex on the brain (some more than others), but sometimes you're interested in sharing more of your life with someone, other than just what you have to offer physically or casually.

Sometimes, if you want the romantic relationship, it is a great idea to head more into the realm of the long-term relationship-centric online dating websites. These are the ones that boast high percentages of long-term relationships and also marriages among users.

BE HONEST WITH YOURSELF, AND WITH THE OTHER PERSON.

The two of you will need to be exceptionally honest with one another throughout the entire relationship. Be sure to ask the hard and pointed questions about whether or not this is just a casual affair or if it is something that you both think will progress into a long lasting, exclusive relationship. It is incredibly important to not wait too long to ask these questions of one another; make it a point to obtain immense clarity on the subject while you are still friendly and casual with one another, rather than romantically entrenched. If tension builds and these issues are left unresolved, it can lead to some serious resentment and the wish that you had better explained the situation earlier on.

POP QUIZ TIME!

Ask yourself these few questions to see where you land on the dating map:

- Are you prepared for a guy to say "no sleepovers?" after a casual encounter? Will you freak out?
- The new guy you really like and have made out with on numerous occasions stops returning your phone calls. How do you feel?
- You've just finished dinner and a few drinks, at midnight. He says: "So, do you want to come back to my place?" What do you envision happening there?
- Your answers to these questions will be extremely telling as to whether or not you are looking for something more casual, or if you're attempting to be in this relationship for the long haul. As always, choose wisely and make the decision that makes you feel happiest and most in tune with your deepest desires and fulfillment.

Chapter 3: Maneuvering Through the Dynamics of Dating

The only things more certain in life than all of the distinct differences between men and women are death and taxes. You'll never be surprised to hear that the two genders didn't see eye-to-eye on something or that a man expected one thing and a woman expected another. If we all understood one another perfectly well every time we interacted, there would be a lot of matchmakers and matchmaking online dating services put out of business. To be successful in online dating, it's truly important to understand how the dynamics of dating between a man and a woman tend to play out online.

Sometimes, it feels as though men don't even consider half of the things we women find to be incredibly important in terms of cultivating and building relationships. Our minds are built somewhat differently, but fundamentally, we do all want to achieve happiness, so our best bet is to figure out how to make everyone happy. Contrary to popular belief, compromise and understanding can at least have us all well within reach of a common denominator. It is crucial to be tolerant, and to know how to handle yourself and what to expect and not expect as you travel from profile searching, sending messages, to dates and beyond.

UNDERSTAND WHERE CHIVALRY LANDS ONLINE.

It can be totally confusing to figure out how each of you are meant to act within the online dating setting. One of the nice things about it though, is that you automatically know that there is an initial romantic intent to the relationship you're building, since it's based in this online dating website. Whether or not your relationship becomes strictly platonic will obviously depend on the level of chemistry between you and your prospective mate. However, if you are a more traditional woman, be aware that many aspects of the courteous behavior a man extends towards a woman can often times take a backseat in this more leveled playing field:

You will sometimes have to send the first message.

Don't freak out just yet! I know that it may seem as if chivalry is dead, but right along with the innovation of online dating comes the idea of occasionally throwing what's traditionally acceptable right out the window. You can't build a great profile and then wait around for someone else to message you every single time. It's not impossible that sometimes, a guy that you actually think has a pretty great profile is a tad bit shy, and may not make the first move with every girl.

Don't get me wrong; I'm not saying to enable every lazy dater you come along, but it's often a pleasant surprise to take the pressure off of a man who is expected to always spark the first contact between himself and a potential match. I have definitely sent a first message to a man (nowadays, more often than not because I know what I want and I grab the opportunity) and I know each time it was thoroughly appreciated. Sometimes nothing came of it, but sometimes I met someone really cool!

And I've even done it in real life. I met my last great boyfriend by walking up to him on a particularly amazing night out with friends and, amidst countless dates I had made online and feeling outrageously confident, I stepped right up to him and engaged him in a conversation. The effort you put into being proactive will reward you tenfold in the long run. It is just one of the many ways in which online dating works as a confidence booster. If I could send someone a silly, flirty message on the Internet and they responded well and promptly—without the pressure of being face to face and forced to answer—surely I could elicit at least a hello from a hottie at the bar.

When you decide where to meet, it may not always be in your neck of the woods.

Though I am a huge proponent of meeting where the lady lives for the sake of her sense of safety and level of comfort, on occasion you may have to meet at a halfway point or go to a neighborhood where neither of you live out of mutual convenience. Being a metropolitan woman has taught me how to deal with this in spades, since trying to decide which "town" to meet up in on a first date could very well mean I'd be sitting on a train for an hour, or longer. Usually, men are pretty receptive and compassionate towards dealing with your level of hesitance, but try to be accommodating as well and don't make it so that they're taking a ridiculously long trek, either.

Be prepared to have a couple great ideas for a bar or take recommendations from friends, if you're having a difficult time deciding on a locale. Also, be prepared to go home alone after a date and possibly drunk. If you live the city life as I do, and have made the (intelligent) decision to not spend the night at every single date's apartment after meeting up, you'll have to be very smart and very careful about getting yourself home safely. Most importantly, be prepared to acclimate yourself to a neighborhood that you're unfamiliar with; you may need to reprogram your stubborn ways and quit being a princess!

You'll occasionally be asked to split the bill.

I'm sure this has happened to plenty of you already, in your regular dating lives, but I feel as though this is an issue that is definitely more prevalent when it comes to dating online. Perhaps it is due to the mutually invested nature of the date: most of the time when you meet in the regular everyday setting, one person will ask another person out on the date, and the person who asks is expected to pay. This can and will often hold true in online dating, as well. However, it's more often a simultaneous decision to meet up (even if one person extends the invitation first).

This definitely doesn't mean that you'll never get a fellow who isn't adamant about footing the entire bill! That happens often too, especially if he is particularly attracted to you and thinks that you both could work out well together in the long run. He will think of it as an investment, and all the more power to him! You just need to ensure that you don't *expect* it every single time. If you're feeling particularly sporting, get used to the idea of fair pay.

Here is a helpful tip, in any situation: if you've invited the guy out on a date and come to realize you aren't as interested in him as you hoped, you should at least offer to foot the entire bill. If he invited you out and you aren't having a good time, paying for whatever drinks or other items you are responsible for can be a silent but effective way of saying "thanks, but I'll take care of my own expenses since I'm not too interested and I don't want to feel beholden to you." If you decide to pay your way but *do* actually like the guy, make sure you use other cues that make it obvious that you're independent but still very much interested!

KNOW THAT SOME MEN WILL NEED AN EXTRA PUSH.

In addition to chivalry being somewhat outdated in the online dating setting, you need to remember that, just as in real life, some men will need an extra nudge to get the hints that you are really into them, or are at all interested. It can be just as difficult for them to meet a great girl, or they can be inundated by tons of dates that go absolutely nowhere, so make it a point to show him that you're interested (if you are). Using your own brand of body language, smiling at him and engaging his interests or hinting towards another date are all great ways of accomplishing this.

KNOW THAT SOME MEN MIGHT BE INCREDIBLY PUSHY.

Of course, there will always be the men who send you a message that at first sounds incredibly charming and assertive, but it just so turns out that they're really good at trying to force you out on a date with them. Don't buy it, ladies! If you're smart enough to not stand for this in real life, there's no reason why you should do so online. Many people find it is easier to be brazen and bold over the internet because it isn't face-to-face contact. But never forget: online dating is no excuse to knowingly give a total jerk a chance. You'll be setting a poor precedent, as once this kind of guy knows that he can elicit a positive response from his impolite advances, he will never cease that behavior.

FEAR OF REJECTION = AUTOMATIC FAILURE

If you go into your online dating experience terrified of being rejected by someone, you may as well stop reading right now. It is virtually *impossible* to never once be rejected by a guy on an online dating site, for a variety of reasons. They may meet someone else before they really get to know you better, or they could realize that there is some kind of crazy relationship deal breaker; perhaps you only brush your teeth once a day and they go for three! Or, the most dreaded of them all: they simply don't find you attractive. God forbid. Well ladies, it happens. The important thing here is to remember that this happens everyday in real life, except someone doesn't have to ignore your wink, or your message, because we don't have to send those to people in our everyday lives.

If you have a crippling fear of rejection, it will drive you completely insane and make you completely miserable to write a thoughtful, heartfelt message and notice that, while Tim viewed said message, he never responded. Your best bet is to grow a very thick skin; not only will this "rejection" help you grow more powerful and successful in getting used to online dating, but it will strengthen the life-changing characteristic within you; the one that allows you to dive in head first and not be so apprehensive, to be fearless rather than hesitant and worried about the little things.

Chapter 4:Show and Tell!

It's plain to see that this topic is HUGE. It's time to say "HELLO WORLD," and really examine how you would like your online profile to look. How many pictures will you post of yourself? Do you want it your profile to be more serious or more humorous? Basically, what you need to ask yourself is, what vibe do you want to be sending out, as well as determining what kind of man you hope to attract with it. How well you craft your profile, as well as how authentic it is, will determine your success in online dating.

Your online dating profile is your self-advertising billboard. You are not a product, of course, but your profile needs to be treated almost as if it is a romantic resume. It should be like your greatest hits! Truthful, but flattering, your profile shouldn't give you anxiety, but just act as a brief and honest guide to you. Your online dating profile will help a person determine two things: from the pictures, they will gather whether or not they are attracted to you and from the profile text they will see if they find you interesting as well as seeking compatibility.

YOUR PICTURES

CHOOSE 3-5 PICTURES

No one can get a great idea of what someone looks like with only one picture to go off of. Even if the picture is superb, it is really still a nice gesture to have a few of them at the ready, so that potential matches can get a full idea of the kind of person you are from all angles (pun intended). These guys will also want to make sure that you are in fact as attractive as you seem and that it wasn't just a lucky shot that was taken. Also, if you only use one breathtaking picture, it may look as though you're a fake and you couldn't find any more awesome pictures of this mystery girl.

So here's what you should do: try having a few pictures that are stationary, meaning you're standing around doing nothing, perhaps posed. Then, you should keep a couple action shots and candid pictures where you aren't hamming it up for the camera. Finally, if you have some really good stuff, professional shots are fine, but remember that it can also be somewhat pretentious as well as a bit intimidating to have *every* image be picture-perfect. Try to come off as flawless and you'll likely get even less men willing to message you as they may not think they stand a chance. Isn't that ironic?

MAKE SURE THE PHOTOS ARE FLATTERING, BUT ACCURATE.

I know you look amazing in that picture from your cousin's Bachelorette party, and it can be outrageously tempting to use, even if it looks absolutely nothing like you. But here I am, and I'm telling you: DON'T DO IT. Sure, it really is a great shot, but the last thing you want is to have this ridiculously stunning picture of yourself online, only to disappoint your date when you meet them in person for the first time. Do you really want to see a look of dismay on your date's face as you're walking up to them in the bar?

Many women suffer from low self-esteem, and there are ridiculous standards out in our society, attempting to force us to be some incredibly unattainable model status kind of girl. This is the time to really look within yourself and find the courage to put your best face out there, even if you have imperfections that make you somewhat uncomfortable. What you need to realize is that if your eyes are far apart, or you have what some might consider to be a big nose, whether you like it or not a guy that you meet with for a date will see it.

If you believe that you can fool someone into going on a date with you by posting a cleverly shot picture online and getting him to meet up, you're in for a world of heartache when he politely continues the date but never calls you again. If you begin your first encounter by being less than truthful, what kind of message do you think that will that send in terms of how honest you'll be in the long-term? If there is something about you that you don't like, feel free to not highlight it. If you think that wearing a little bit of makeup in a photo will make you come across a bit more photogenic that's totally fine as well.

To add to that, look on the bright side: imagine that you have some kind of physical self esteem issue, you put yourself out there and you receive a positive response from a guy who actually seems pretty nice. It's kind of a great self esteem booster as well as positive reinforcement that you're probably stressing too much. Even though we are the more forgiving of the sexes in the looks department, many, many men can be surprisingly less shallow than we imagine they are. So in closing, there are so many flattering ways to take a picture without using smoke and mirrors and all sorts of illusions to make yourself look way better or far different than you actually do. Your date will appreciate the honesty.

YOUR PICTURES NEED TO BE RECENTLY TAKEN AS WELL.

We women are known for taking great strides toward anti-aging and looking perfect at all times, but just as you don't want to give the wrong impression with a flattering picture that doesn't look like you, make sure your photo is up to date. Don't post a picture from two years ago and then be insulted when your date notices that you're 15 pounds heavier. You wouldn't appreciate him doing that to you, so I suggest you don't do it to him. Really let someone know what they're in for, and what to expect.

CLOSE-UPS AND FULL-BODY SHOTS ONLY!

Most sites won't let you put up pictures of your dog, or a cartoon anyway, but it should go without saying that it is a waste of time to put up any pictures in your main profile space that aren't of you. The impression is gives is that you are trying to hide something, and that is never good for a first impression. It is also common courtesy to include an accurate, full body shot so that potential dates are aware of your body type. Again, this isn't based on rudeness or intrusiveness, it is simply about projecting exactly who you are to the guys you meet. In keeping with that sentiment, don't post a picture of you in a bikini from the neck down and then act surprised if a guy focuses solely on that picture and messages you inappropriately. Treat yourself with respect and tune the focus to *all* of you, and men will take the hint.

SMILE FOR THE CAMERA!

Profile pictures where you are smiling will win people over, every single time. Men and women alike are more attracted to smiling pictures because it shows a sense of humor and an ability to not take yourself too seriously that EVERYONE can appreciate. Again, it is all about being able to show your best face to the men you hope to meet, and letting them know that if they play their cards right, they too can make you smile.

SHOW THEM WHAT YOU VALUE.

Your profile pictures should definitely give a glimpse into your personality. Whether it be your choice of clothing, or an action shot of you diving off a cliff in New Mexico, you really do want this picture to say a thousand words.

DON'T SHARE THE SPOTLIGHT WITH A GIRLFRIEND.

What if the man of your dreams finds her more attractive?! Maybe that's a little far-fetched, but it is totally, 100% possible. Either way, the focus should be 100% on YOU. It is your profile, anyway, and you don't want any distractions from you. That doesn't mean that you should go forth and find your most conventionally unattractive friend, either. Take *your* best pictures and go forth into the wonderful world of online dating!

YOUR PROFILE TEXT

TREAT IT LIKE A RESUME.

In the regular world, your resume is a showcase of the best of what you've done; it helps people understand your strengths, your interests, and why you're a great candidate. Obviously, your online dating profile isn't very different at all.

KEEP IT BRIEF!

Don't make your profile too long. *Yawn.* While you now know that having a profile that is too short doesn't give enough information about you and doesn't appear well thought out, be aware that a profile that is too long gives the impression of someone who is a complete talker and not at all a listener. Remember that in many cases, the pictures will be the true deciding factor and the profile just the icing on the cake. So be *pithy* with your profile—that is to say, be *concise* and be *expressive*.

BE THE WOMAN YOU ARE, INSTEAD OF THE WOMAN YOU THINK A MAN WANTS YOU TO BE.

Pretending to be someone you are not can be a difficult and tiring act to keep up. At some point in your relationship, you'll grow weary of being entirely on your best behavior, or having lied and said you love his favorite movie, when really, you can hardly stand it. Don't try and tailor your profile to suit the whims of a man you think you're after. You want someone who wants to date you unconditionally, whether it is a casual relationship or a long-term one. Not only is this healthier, but you can bet it is a million times more rewarding and an overall great feeling when a genuine profile that reflects exactly who you are, catches the eye of an awesome man.

TELL THESE MEN WHAT YOU DO WELL.

In keeping with being the woman you are, you want to let every guy know what you've excelled at in life. Just as a woman wants a talented man, a man wants a woman who stands out from the crowd as well. Is it a career success, or a longstanding personal goal that you've achieved? Whatever it is, it will express that you get *results* and everyone finds that attractive.

SHARE WHAT REALLY INTERESTS YOU.

What are you passionate about in general? Maybe it is a hobby, or something you've yet to explore and you're looking for someone to do it with. The greatest part of reading profiles is when you find someone you think you can truly connect with, and the best way to do that is when you see what kinds of interests you have in common. So make them known!

UPDATE YOUR PROFILE FREQUENTLY.

Don't feel like you're being insincere if you frequently update your profile. Things change all the time—you may even need to take it down temporarily or permanently, if you meet a great person! But is it important to keep your pictures, location, stats and interests up to date, so that you don't have an awkward moment where someone messages you and realizes that you no longer have the same, awe-inducing dedication to skydiving that you once did. Additionally, on many sites, updating your profile regularly causes you to come in higher on the search, so you'll definitely be rewarded with more profile views! It really is a win-win situation.

Other really important reasons/opportunities to keep it fresh?

1. If you look dramatically different.
2. If you're unhappy about the amount of responses you're getting from potential dates.

Chapter 5: Advance and Avoid: The Honest Do's and Don'ts

You need to be aware of the rules of online dating backwards and forwards. Pay attention to the light bulbs that go off as well as the warning signs, to ensure that your online dating experience is a happy and healthy one.

CREATE A SUREFIRE LIST OF HARD AND FAST QUALITIES THAT YOUR MAN MUST HAVE.

Is he active? Mark it. Does he enjoy reading regularly? Make that mental notation. You're allowed to have a *few* hard and fast, general characteristics that help you narrow down the vast options and sheer amount of profiles that online dating has to offer. Just remember, don't go crazy with a super long, unforgiving list! If you're too rigid and picky, you shouldn't be surprised when you've tapped the proverbial well entirely.

ONCE IN A WHILE, IT'S OKAY TO NOT RESPOND

Sounds crazy, right? Well, it is kind of expected online that occasionally, if someone sends you a first contact and you're just not interested, it's easier to not say anything at all. No harm, no foul. Receiving a response with a full on rejection may do more harm than good. Me personally? I would rather just not know. At the beginning you'll find it hard to never hear back from certain guys, or to not respond to a really sincere message from someone you totally know you're just not into. But sometimes? Ignorance is truly bliss.

MAKE THE MOST OF THE INTERNAL SEARCH ENGINE.

Once you have a brief list of sure fires, the search engine is a great way to help you harness a ton of profiles with whatever interest you have chosen. The best way to use it is to utilize the keyword search options. If a potential match has the keyword in their profile, it can often give you a great insight into their personality. One of my recent keyword searches was an interest in Muay Thai kickboxing. Muay Thai is a particularly strenuous contact sport and it takes a lot of discipline to truly excel at it. For that reason, I found that it was a great indicator of a man who was not only interesting in staying in shape, but also maintaining a solid and challenging routine.

LEARN HOW TO TREAD THAT FINE LINE BETWEEN BEING OVERZEALOUS AND PLAYING HARD TO GET.

One of the hardest things to figure out in online dating, can be how long to wait before sending out a message. It is clear that you don't want to respond with lightning speed every single time a guy sends you a note (appearing desperate or needy), but you also don't want to linger too long on them either (losing some much-needed momentum). This is definitely a time when you want to learn your own balance. A helpful hint: if it takes you a little bit of time to come up with a clever or well-thought out message or response, let that time take its course. Waiting an entire day definitely loses steam, but a few hours are a pretty healthy choice. Regardless of how long you wait or do not wait, a good match will be a good match, and two interested parties will be hot on the trail.

BE CRYSTAL CLEAR AT ALL TIMES.

It is not in your best interest to beat around the bush. You need to be clear about what you want, as it is already difficult to gauge certain personality cues online. This is also where it helps to make certain you are getting the point across in regards to more fun and flirty relationships or something in the long term. The more straightforward you are in your profile, the more likely you are to avoid messages from men who you're really not all that interested in. Remember, it is important to be pithy and express a lot of information in fewer words.

REMEMBER THAT THE CONNOTATION OF YOUR TEXT CAN SOMETIMES LEAD TO CONFUSION.

We all know how text can be misconstrued, like how a more or less harmless but sarcastic text message can be misinterpreted as a seriously bitchy one. Silly though it may seem, it is really quite important to utilize emoticons and exclamation points to convey a humorous and good-natured message. If you want to be sarcastic or cynical in a friendly way, overdo it on the hyperbole and exaggerate a bit. Make sure that it can't possibly be mistaken as something catty. That kind of miscommunication could lose a great match opportunity!

ACTIVELY AVOID BEING BAITED BY "PICK-UP ARTISTS".

The Pick-Up Artist is one of the most unfortunate types within the male breed. This is a guy who considers himself a master at attracting and seducing a woman, usually better known as a player. Call it whatever you need to, but note his lousy and uninspired tricks, which include:

a. <u>Sending you a message that is incredibly vague and makes no mention of anything specifically regarding you.</u>

The effort being expended by this "gentleman" is little to none. He may have changed a name, or a location, but this message is absolutely premade. Players create premade messages and send them out to prospective dates in the same manner that someone might copy and paste the same cover letter onto a resume and send it out to multiple prospective employers. It is completely impersonal and highly inconsiderate, so avoid this like the plague.

Casual relationship or not, this is insulting. Even if your relationship is purely sexual, you should feel respected; encouraging the laziness of a player and allowing him to lump you in with whomever else he's "courting" will set a poor precedent. Always know your worth.

b. His message includes an insult masked as a compliment to subconsciously make you seek out his approval.

Again, know your worth! Any guy who is daft enough to mask a compliment with an insult in order to get your attention is likely insecure, not to mention immature. Typically, someone who feels that they have to compliment another person indirectly is not comfortable with the idea of telling someone how awesome they are outright. That is the kind of thing that undeveloped gentlemen can find daunting, as if it is a great commitment to express to someone how you feel.

If the guy you have your sights set on can't be honest and tell you he likes something about you, without thinking it is a shot to his manhood or that he will be seen as "soft" or overly-sensitive, it is not worth it to keep him around.

- **The only time you hear from him is on *his terms*.**

You should never feel as though you're being manipulated by any male you're seeing. Here's a great example: you call or text the man in question one night, asking him to hang out and he either completely ignores you or declines your invitation, however politely. This continues to happen on a very regular basis. *YET,* when he extends an invitation, he expects you to be free and/or is frustrated when you aren't. Furthering this, because you are interested, you make it a point to see him when he messages you, but this behavior will only be to your detriment, and I'm going to tell you why.

First of all, if you're only seeing a guy when *he* decides he's free to see you, it's likely because he's juggling plenty of events/dates/casual encounters and the random times you throw at him don't work well with his obviously busy schedule. He maintains control of his situation by being the deciding factor in when he sees

36

everyone with whom he is involved. But do you only want to see a guy when *he* is willing and available? Are you a lap dog, willing to come whenever he calls? Definitely not.

Of course, to be fair, there is always the possibility that a guy is genuinely busy whenever you'd like to see him, and coincidentally, you are free whenever he asks, but it is highly unlikely. Your best bet is to bring up this discrepancy with him and see if his behavior and schedule changes to suit you as often as yours suits him. Never turn a one-sided hook up into a habit.

DON'T LET A MAN GUILT YOU INTO ANY MEETING OR SENDING HIM THINGS—*ANYTHING*.

This is extremely important! If you learn only a few things from this online dating guide tailored specifically for the fairer sex, let this be one of them. This journey into online dating is your powerful, independent and headstrong endeavor, so the worst thing you could possibly do is make a grave misstep and let a man you meet online overpower you. As I've mentioned, it is truly easy for someone to take on a pushier, more aggressive persona when they are not directly in front of someone. People can masquerade as whoever they want behind a computer screen, but it isn't always for the better.

Never let anyone dehumanize you in any way, whether it is manipulating you into going on a date with them, sending sexy or half-nude photos against your better judgment, or even continuing a conversation that you no longer have any interest in, especially if that conversation is of a sexual nature. You may think that it is quite harmless because you too are behind a computer screen, but don't be fooled—your actions could have serious repercussions.

BE *OUTRAGEOUSLY* DISCERNING. THERE ARE NO HONESTY POLICE IN ONLINE DATING.

This is in keeping with what I just mentioned about people masquerading as whomever they want on the internet. What do I mean by be *outrageously* discerning? It means that you need to use your instincts and remove yourself from ANY situation or burgeoning relationship that makes you at all uncomfortable. It means confronting someone if you catch them in a lie, and being 100% aware that sometimes, even if you think someone is great, they can be a total liar and even a predator. It is so incredibly important to keep yourself safe, because the "Honesty Police" don't exist, and no one can investigate your potential matches better than you.

It goes without saying that you should keep all of your personal information to yourself until you are absolutely comfortable sharing any of it with a potential date.

GAUGE COMPATIBILITY QUICKLY

The sooner you figure out whether or not a guy is worth your time, the sooner you can either catch his eye and/or ask him out, or just quit looking at his profile and move on to the next great opportunity. Don't waste a lot of time convincing yourself that someone might be cool; there is a difference between being open-minded and if the excitement is there, it is easy to see. If you're not excited about the match, it will show, and it will be a waste of time.

DON'T BUILD HIM UP, BUTTERCUP.

Remember that people can be different in person than they are on paper. It is one thing to be super psyched up to meet a guy, but don't start fantasizing about your marriage vows before you even meet him! Riding all of your hopes and dreams on one fellow will totally bite you in the ass in the long run. This can happen at any point in the prospective dating scene.

a. You look at his profile and it looks absolutely perfect, but then he never replies back to the message you sent him.
b. You make it past the message round, but after a few amazing exchanges, you never hear from him again.
c. You even make it to the first date, and think everything went swimmingly, but never hear from him again.

Noticing the trend in the first three instances? You don't want to me a miserable wreck if you never hear from your "dream guy" again. At the beginning of a relationship, there may be any number of reasons for why he didn't return your message/call.

And actually, there is one more occasion for which you shouldn't get overexcited and make put him on a pedestal *before* you meet.

You meet up with this man who you've built up in your mind for the first time, and it turns out he's nothing like what you imagined.

I refer to this as Crush Syndrome. Crushes are a funny thing, because you meet someone quite vaguely and construct an idea of their personality and behavior based on your ideal of the perfect person. Little do you realize, the more you get to know them, the more they end up being completely different from what you've fabricated.

MAKE SURE YOU UTILIZE FREE SITES!

Free sites will be one of your greatest allies in the online dating championship. This is not to say that pay sites cannot get you great results, but there are tons of free sites with normal, awesome people just like you, so make good use of them first and see what you discover. The money you save on membership fees can be used towards nights out, or awesome outfits to wear on all of your dates! Plus, using a pay site could spawn resentment if for some reason you don't feel like you're getting your money's worth, which is completely subjective. I personally have had great success with free sites.

Chapter 6: Exploration: Seeking Out Prospects

This is where things get really exciting! It's time to be your own "heat"-seeking missile! You want to find the man of your dreams, or of the moment. FURTHERMORE, you want to enjoy yourself while doing so. A wise person once said, "with great numbers of online dating profiles, come greatly overwhelmed women". At least, I think that's what they said. However you slice it, you need to be prepared to flip through an ocean of profiles and keep your options wide open, while remembering what you most value in a match. Don't worry woman, I'm here to guide you.

FISH FOR AS MANY MEN AS YOU CAN CATCH.

Answer this question honestly: why *wouldn't* you seek out as many potential dates as you possibly could? Online, the odds are in your favor. Yes, you are narrowing down the pool with your list of surefire qualities (as well as maintaining a highly discerning outlook in regards to compatibility) but reading countless profiles will give you a broad array of choices, expanding not only your search but your knowledge base of the opposite sex. Take note of the similarities and differences within all of these profiles and use it to further tailor what it is that you are looking for in an awesome guy!

KEEP YOUR MIND (AND YOUR CALENDAR) BUSY WITH THE SEARCH.

This will help you from plotting only one man on your radar and making this singular prospect far too precious. You don't want to be devastated if you never receive any response from this guy, or if it turns out that he's not exactly what you first envisioned. Keeping yourself from focusing too much on one person by engaging in various messages and flirtatious exchanges will keep you from being seriously disappointed if the primary subject drops out. It's great to keep the ball rolling nonstop on these because you can almost never anticipate when a budding online relationship will falter. Additionally, the concentrated juggling will be a good tool to use in your real life! Ever tried to balance a ridiculous amount of projects and feel the heat? Here's a fun, sexy way to train you!

BOOKMARK TONS OF ELIGIBLE PROFILES.

Don't have enough time to completely scroll through a profile that looks promising right at that exact moment? Save it in your web browser to check it out later! Or better yet, add it to your favorites within the website, since some online dating sites notify users if they've been added to someone's Favorites List. That in itself is an absolute great way to show someone that you're interested when you don't exactly have enough time to send a well thought out message.

ENGAGE HIM WITH YOUR FIRST MESSAGE.

So you're ready to send your first peep! Whether it is the first contact message sent out to a new prospect, or you're replying to someone else's first contact message, keep it interesting enough to pique his interest in responding to you, or to prove that he made a great choice in contacting you in the first place.

a. <u>Don't send a superbly generalized message!</u>

A "Hi, What's up?" will certainly not get you far. I remember how I cringed every time I received one of those from some guy. Did he even care? Did he just copy and paste that into every message he sent?

b. <u>Don't give it all away in one shot.</u>

Avoid telling someone your entire life story in your first message. You need to give them time to get to know you, and if you say it all to begin with, what else is there to learn? You'll feel as though you've already been on a number of dates with this person and they were kind of boring too, I bet. So think twice before you detail where you live and enumerate every single thing you do in your spare time, along with how many pets you want to own someday and a guided tour of your life plan.

c. <u>Don't go overboard.</u>

Try not to hit the nail over the head too many times, in terms of say, giving him compliments. It seems forced and somewhat artificial when you send a message like "Wow! You are amazingly cute! Blah blah blah I can't imagine a super hottie like you bothering to be on this website!" Everyone likes to be complimented, but it might be a little much and it may be laying it on too thick to throw down that much appreciation before you actually meet this person in real life.

d. <u>Know your worth.</u>

This can often especially be difficult for ladies who suffer from low self esteem, but sending a message that reads similarly to "Blah blah blah, answer my message if you think you're interested," doesn't read confidently in the least! Listen: everyone loves confidence in their mate, whether they know it or not. It is an innate requirement within our DNA, and even if you aren't dating Captain America, you are dating him because he is at least confident in the fact that he deserves to be dating you, and vice versa. When that doesn't happen, a relationship is bound for disaster. So, if nothing else, come across a strong candidate deserving of love and attention.

e. <u>Don't try to hard to be interesting</u>.

It's good to stand out and to be quirky, but don't let it get out of hand. For example, if you're funny, that's great and fantastic for you, but laying it on too thick might not translate well through a text message format. Again, we must always remember the ramifications of misunderstood connotation. Also, as a girl, everyone wants to label you as crazy anyway, so if your first message says something along the lines of "HALLO THERE, HOTTIE. TIME TO PARTY.", you may think that's hilarious, but I'll bet on my life he's backing away from his computer, very slowly, wondering exactly how often in which you go from cool to psycho in fifteen seconds.

f. Don't play coy.

Don't add someone to your favorites list or send them a wink without actually saying a word to them. It's a huge copout; have the proverbial balls to send a true first message.

g. Be sure that the message you send is left open ended.

Make sure that you end every message you send either with a question, or some interesting and conversation-starting piece of information that the guy you're chatting with can latch on to. Conversations are a two way street, and so you shouldn't leave him hanging, trying to pull some interesting chat out of thin air.

h. Fit in a few questions of your own.

In keeping with leaving open ended messages, be sure to ask your important, discerning questions early on, so that you can weed out potential matches that are incompatible. He doesn't like to read and you have a library of one thousand books? Maybe you're no longer interested. He thinks that women have an obligation to shave their legs and yours haven't seen a razor in six years? Kind of obvious.

BE SURE TO KEEP THEM ALL STRAIGHT!

Sometimes it seems this can be more of an issue for a pick-up artist/player but when you're swimming in conversations, it can become difficult to keep everyone's story straight! If you need to keep a cheat sheet somewhere, just do it. Or, if you need to review old messages, make it so; nothing is worse than mixing up someone's information and leading them to believe that you couldn't care less about the conversation the both of you are having. We're all human, so we are definitely subject to occasional forgetfulness. Just as many women find it incredibly thoughtful when a man remembers something subtle about them, any guy will appreciate if you remembered what basketball team he rooted for last weekend, for instance.

Chapter 7: Up On Your Feet: The Guide to the First Date and Beyond

All of your hard work and effort culminate in the first date. When you meet in person for the first time, you should be calm, cool and collected. Nervousness, anxiousness and worry shouldn't even factor in! Make the best impression face to face and have an awesome time whether there are fireworks or not!

DON'T EXPECT TOO MUCH ON THE FIRST DATE!

Even if you are really excited about a guy, don't go into the first date expecting it to be the most amazing date you've ever been on. As with anything in life, if your expectations are too high, sometimes you're just bound to be disappointed. When you keep these expectations at a practical level, you'll be able to look at the situation much more objectively. Plus, you won't feel as if you've been on a string of terrible dates that more than likely *weren't* so terrible. Your first date goals should simply involve the following:

a. <u>Meeting face to face for the first time.</u>

b. <u>Seeing what it's like to hang out together and how your personalities mesh (or don't).</u>

c. <u>Engaging in some sort of activity—a movie, a picnic or a concert perhaps.</u>

LOOK YOUR BEST, BUT DRESS COMFORTABLY!

There are few things that could be more of a pain in the butt than not feeling 100% fabulous on your first date. When you are meeting someone for the first time, you don't want to be worried about whether or not your top is too low cut, your clothes don't fit right, or if your skirt is just plain too short. You should be focused solely on having an enjoyable time, and the kind of anxiety inducing debate over what you'll be wearing will make for a disastrous date. You won't be able to hear what he's saying over your subconscious telling you that you're overdressed.

Make sure that you test-drive whichever outfit you choose before you wear it out to meet up with a new guy. Even better: make sure ahead of time that you know what kind of event you're attending so that you can dress accordingly. It would really be a shame if you wore heels and a mini dress to say, a stadium seating baseball game.

PARTICIPATE IN GENUINE SMILES AND LAUGHTER.

Even if you're absolutely positive during the first date that this new man isn't creating butterflies in your stomach, that's no excuse to be completely awkward for the duration of the date. Smiles and laughter do a lot to ease tension, and both can be a great for your mutual benefit. We know that every single date we go on won't be a home run but it's still nice to experience a good time with someone. Human connection and interaction can never be replaced, so even though it was the internet that helped you secure your date in the first place, always remember that ultimately, it's all about the healthy relationships you are building with real people in real time.

EAT WHATEVER THE HELL YOU WANT.

This should really go without saying, but I feel as though women are still conditioned to not want to pig out in the company of a man that they find attractive. Any man who judges you based on what you're eating needs to mind his own business. Honestly, a good deal of the self-consciousness that arises during eating whatever you want stems from an internal unhappiness. Are you uncomfortable with your body? Then you might be more likely to not want to gobble down a hamburger in front of your potential boyfriend.

This also draws from the idea of not trying to portray yourself as a person you are not. How long do you intend to keep up the charade of eating like a small, woodland creature when all you really want to do is scarf down carbohydrates? Ask yourself that, and ask yourself if you really want to be with someone who turns up his nose at a woman with an appetite. I also find that sometimes it's actually quite evident from someone's profile that they're either the kind of male who is easygoing in that regard or may be more uptight about it even from their profile.

SKIP THE SMALL TALK.

I guarantee you; men will appreciate the heck out of this. Really grab a hold of the meat and potatoes of your conversations. After all, the first couple of dates are like mutual interviews, seeing how well you get along with this person and what you have in common. There is a difference between politeness and boringness. Obviously, you're not going to want to start investigating about his past girlfriends, but you also don't want to keep the conversation of a tedious, strictly talking about "work and the weather" sort of nature.

Conversely, don't be too talkative either. Women talk more then men—by *nature*, I haven't made up this statistic—so take a breath and let him get a word in edgewise! You want this to be a good balance of give and take, otherwise you'll make it to the end of the date realizing that you really don't know that much about him, and possibly not nearly enough to make an educated decision on whether or not you'd like to partake of a second date.

LEAVE THE PHONE ALONE.

I will be the first person to admit: this is incredibly difficult for me! I am attached at the hip to my phone, literally, and feel like I have to be on top of every single thing and aware of all emails and text messages at every waking moment. However, it is really important to give your guy your undivided attention. It's almost as bad as talking nonstop because everyone deserves to feel like they're being listened to.

Consider it this way: if I'm on a date with a guy and he is checking his phone non-stop, I start thinking that whatever he's checking is more important than me, and wondering if maybe he's setting up his next date with another woman! Don't give your date a reason to think you're that rude and unappreciative of their time. If you think it might be an emergency, go for it. If not, really try to leave your phone in your bag or pocketbook.

If you're good at being stealthy, you're allowed to check it while your date is in the restroom, but only for a split second! It must go back in the bag before they arrive back at your table (or other venue), and if it isn't urgent, you don't need to respond to any messages that have arrived since the date began.

ALWAYS BE EARLY (OR AT LEAST ON TIME).

The advantage to showing up to your date early is that you get an imaginary home-court advantage – you're settled in, not feeling rushed and you even get to preview your date's behavior if you manage to spot them first. Rushing because you're late will leave you feeling flustered, unprepared, and obviously doesn't make for the best first impression.

To prepare for the sad, sad event that you do happen to be late for your date, choose a spot that is filled with people. Aside from the fact that it is clearly safer, it is easier to meet where there are a lot of people to distract your date from playing the waiting game in your absence.

DON'T DRINK TOO MUCH.

Not only is it unattractive to be a sloppy drunk, but it leaves you susceptible to very poor decision making! I know that sometimes a little liquid courage may seem helpful, but there is a canyon of difference between a single drink to loosen you up and getting completely and utterly intoxicated before you meet up with your date, or over the course of the date. You don't want this guy to be incredibly embarrassed from trying to figure out how to get you home in one piece. You also don't want to be taken advantage of by complete jerk that you would have recognized as a creep whilst sober, but now are too inebriated to evade his unwanted advances.

DON'T TALK ABOUT UNSAVORY ITEMS.

This includes, but is not limited to:

a. <u>Past Relationships/Super Specific Information about Other Dates</u>

This date is strictly about the two of you. Don't sour it by getting into the torrid details of all your other dates gone wrong, or past lovers who did you wrong. Your date will perceive this at you not being over the relationship, or they may see themselves becoming a rebound and feel compelled to steer clear. If it's a very vague, incredibly humorous story, it *might* get a pass, but otherwise, let it go for sure.

b. <u>THEIR Past Relationships/Past Dates</u>

Whatever you do, do not ask pointed questions about your dates past dates and relationships. This is not only incredibly nosy, but it can appear to your date that you can't mind your own business or are insecure. If they volunteer information, it's a bit different, but either way, neither party should be discussing the past on date one.

c. <u>Your illnesses or ones in the family.</u>

This information should be given on a need to know basis, and I doubt your first date needs to know about your Mom's hemorrhoids. Conversely, if you're a diabetic, letting your date know ahead of time that you may need to check your blood sugar is fair game. They deserve to know why all of a sudden you're dizzy and need to be rushed to the nearest supermarket, don't you think?

 d. How Much You Can't Stand Your Job.

You're supposed to be having a great time on your date, so why are you busy discussing the things that make you more or less unhappy? Stay away.

IF YOU'RE INTERESTED, PAVE THE WAY FOR A SECOND DATE.

Don't leave the guy you've just met completely clueless to the fact that you are interested in seeing him again. Even if the first date didn't send fireworks shooting off into the sky, you may want to give it a few dates to see if you'd like to keep each other around. Don't expect him to be a mind reader; even if it's a gesture as small as a text message or a brief phone call right after the date—in fact, try to get confirmation before the date ends—let him know you enjoyed his time and leave him with the hint that an invitation to a follow up date is more than welcome.

One of the best ways to do this is to introduce a mutually desirable activity into the equation during the first day. Say for instance you both were quite looking forward to a new release in the movie theatre—subtly suggest that the two of you see it together. That way, it is quite clear that you like him enough to want to spend more time with him, even though it may not be an instant love connection.

IF YOU'RE *REALLY* INTERESTED, SHOW HIM JUST A TOUCH.

I mean this literally. Show him a T-O-U-C-H. It isn't a crime to get close! And yes, this means even on the first date. There is nothing inherently brazen about using bodily contact or body language to show off your interest. Furthermore, men are much more cognizant of physical cues and it is IMPERATIVE to remember that they aren't mind readers. Whether it's just a brush past him or a gentle shoulder tap after being away for a moment or two, it will make it clear that you feel comfortable enough with him to lay hands.

IF YOU DON'T WANT TO SLEEP WITH HIM, DON'T SLEEP WITH HIM.

This sentiment originates in not doing anything you don't feel comfortable doing. Of course, first and foremost, no man should ever make you feel guilty for not having sex with him or try and coerce you into doing anything against your better judgment. You don't owe him anything. Furthermore, if you don't have any strong feelings there, there's no need to introduce that strong physical bond. If your outlook on dating involves you bedding a man just on a whim, online dating may make you reconsider.

Think about it this way: if you're using online dating in a manner most in keeping with what I've detailed thus far, you'll be going on a *lot* of dates. You're not going to sleep with everyone you meet, but you also shouldn't sleep with the majority. You'll need to be highly discerning on this. Keep your psyche and your physical planes at a respectable and distinguished level.

IF YOU KNOW YOU'RE NOT INTERESTED, DON'T LEAD HIM ON!

Every moderately experienced woman who's been on a couple dates can tell you how unfortunate and hurtful it can feel when you realize you've been lead on by a potential match. If you're slowly falling head over heels for someone and you imagine that the feeling is mutual, only to find out that they have waited weeks (possibly months!) to let you know they don't see a future with you, it can be devastating. You know that it is often less painful to just let a person down gently earlier on than to prolong the heartache.

Although this is often seen as something that men do more often than women, there are more than a few instances where a woman may be apprehensive in regards to telling a man she's not interested, or that it's over. One scenario that is occurs most often involves the nice guy. As a woman, when you meet a man who is genuinely a good guy and isn't a player, you may be less inclined to let him go, since these characteristics lay at the crux of the optimal male. If he doesn't satisfy a majority of your most important requirements, however—say for instance he's also messy and no good at budgeting his finances—it's best that you turn him loose!

DON'T FORGET:

Once you head out for the face to face meet up, your behavior on a date that you've attained through online means shouldn't really differ at all from your behavior on a date you achieved the old fashioned way. After all, the online aspect is just a means to an end; there's no need or reason to treat a person or situation differently because of the manner in which you met.

Sick of the typical dinner and drinks? You've probably been a fan of the dating scene for quite some time. Want some great, unique date ideas to meld perfectly with your great new online dating career? Look no further and mix it up with these fun date ideas, hand-picked by Yours Truly. Good for first dates, second dates and beyond!

1. Grab a bite to eat—but place your date in a venue or restaurant that serves a very specific cuisine!

    Got a serious craving for funnel cake? Find the only place in the city that serves that carnival delight! Or maybe you'd prefer to mutually decide on a specific dish and find the best place in your entire town that serves it up daily. This is a great date because it is a spin on something traditional; there won't be a lot of pressure for it to be perfect (unless you or Mr. Right are banking all of your hopes and dreams on the greatest dinner of their life) and even if the memories of the date don't last, that amazing meal will!

2. Take a walk through the park—stopping to *sketch* along the way.

   You don't have to be a world-class artist to draw what you see all around you. In fact, it would be better if neither of you were any good at making art. Share your not so great looking drawings or inking with one another and prepare to laugh and argue over whose looks worse. This is a great date because it's pretty chilled but it has an activity that will definitely spark conversation, and possibly bring out a different side of you both. If one of you *is* an artist, then you'll score brownie points either by being the proficient one or by providing the proficiency. Everyone knows that knowledge is power; it's also *quite* sexy.

3. Meet up at the library!

   If you're both full of beauty and brains, perusing a bunch of books, or reading your favorite passages to one another from your favorite novels could not only be interesting and enlightening, but incredibly romantic! You'll have to speak quietly, but if you really are into this guy, you'll relish getting close enough to hear one another's whispers, and it will be reward enough to make up for the rules! Similar to the drawing date, this is a great date because it leaves you with something to talk about and no awkward silences. I bet you could probably both go on forever about your favorite Hemingway short story.

4. Explore on a photo-hunt.

   Whip out your cameras and prepare to have a great time! Plan to meet up and snap pictures of whatever you see. Landmarks, interesting statues, artistic shots and of course, even of one another. If you want to do something even cooler, try to decide on a theme and only shoot pictures that relate to it. This is a great date because again, it's a very specific activity without too much pressure and it's nice to embark on an activity that has you acting as partners, in a way that is mutually beneficial. You don't need to have an amazing camera; point and shoots are fine, or even just a camera phone! It's more about engaging one another in this activity.

5. <u>Got a metropolitan public transportation route in your city or town?</u>

Make a train date! Imagine how fun it would be to get to know each other and chat it up while in motion! Especially if you take a route that is atypical for both of you, it will be interesting to explore the location with someone else who hasn't been there and share the experience. It's almost like a trip to the museum except more unique. This is a great date because even when you have those awkward lulls in conversation, if you're lucky enough to be on an above ground train you can just look out the window and find inspiration for something to discuss. Just make sure that you both find seats at some point, or the date will become the worst backache you've ever had. But do you know what the best part is? If you're *not so into* your date, you can hop off at the next stop, never to be seen from again!

6. <u>Go for a hangover brunch.</u>

I know what you're thinking: isn't the idea to be drinking *with* the person that you're dating? Well, wouldn't it be funny if you met up "the morning after" a huge night out, and shared incredulous stories about intoxicated friends and wild cab rides home? Something really tickles my fancy about grabbing a wholesome and tasty brunch after a bender, with someone else who has done the same, just not with you! And hey, isn't it better than meeting up for a brunch with someone who's hung-over when you're definitely not? What a buzz kill.

7. Go shopping!

   There's no better way to learn what someone is into than by being right there with them when they buy it. Again, this date is ultra unconventional, but if you both are in the market for some items, why not? Just don't be the girl who drags a man around a bunch of women's clothing asking silly questions about how it looks and getting upset when he really has no true opinion on it. A scarf is a scarf is a scarf. Conversely, don't let him drag you around looking for golf clubs unless you're super into it as well.

8. Start out with a work out.

   Are you both fit? Are you both fat? Either way, the two of you can join together in health and meet up for a jog! It's a great common interest that you can utilize, and you benefit from some great exercise any way the date happens to go. If one of you belongs to a gym, maybe you can use a friend pass and get the other person in as a show of good faith. For many people, that team effort or friendly competition is a great motivator—myself included. Working out also releases serotonin, as we all know, so it'll probably be a pretty cool date, considering you'll both be very nice to one another.

9. Take your favorite board game to the coffee shop and/or bar.

   Do you have an affinity for *Battleship*? Are you a wordsmith at Scrabble? As long as you're not scarily competitive and don't plan on being a sore loser, playing a game while having drinks at a bar can make for smooth conversational transitions and a fun excuse to get wasted and make fun of each other's dwindling ability to recognize the board beyond the beer goggles. If you know of a cooler game, perhaps one that involves a deck of playing cards, that's also a great icebreaker. This great date gives you the opportunity to show off some serious skill.

10. Strictly Ballroom.

You may think it happens more often, but very rarely does a couple go out specifically to dance. This one might be a little bit more difficult to pull off, considering that not everyone owns a pair of proverbial dancing shoes (especially the guys) but it could be well worth your while. It may also be difficult to find a place that affords great music and dancing but isn't ultra-clubby and full of other single women who may catch your man's eye. However, it's a great excuse to get close if you think you may really have the hots for this fellow.

11. Drag someone special to your very favorite place.

This is another one specifically for someone you think may be pretty special. After all, you wouldn't want to bring some random loser to your all time favorite space, now would you? For whatever reason this place means so much to you—a favorite bar, restaurant, landmark, place to go for whatever kind of activity—it will really get your comfort levels up and when you're more comfortable, you're much better at being yourself around a new person, and further, a new person that you think is attractive. You'll also look pretty cool showing them the ins and outs, so don't be afraid to let them in!

12. Build your own cocktails.

This is one hundred percent a cut to the chase kind of date. If you're either impromptu or self-taught mixologists, this is a great time to open up the liquor cabinet and go to town. It's cheaper than spending a fortune at a bar, and you already know what kind of spirits you like most, so why not? Be prepared though, to get wasted around someone relatively new, but don't let inhibitions run too wild. You know this isn't the date for you if you're a little bit too free and easy when you've been drinking. Use your discretion.

13. Get onto the nearest rooftop and take in the entire landscape.

This is more of a late springtime, full on summertime dating experience. But everyone knows that being on a rooftop on a warm summer night is like heaven. It's fine if the destination is a bar but it's a little bit more exciting if it's someone's rooftop and you have a bit more privacy. Of course, as I've said before, be safe; don't go strolling about on a dangerous roof that lacks guards! But the romance will be on a roof with a great breeze and an amazing view. And it always seems so much quieter up there, doesn't it?

14. Act like a tourist in your own town.

Picture it: you've lived in New York City since you were a wee little child, but never made it to the Statue of Liberty. Or, you're from Philadelphia and never gotten within walking distance of the Liberty Bell. There's always going to be some place in your neighborhood that, despite many (or no) attempts to check out, you really ought to see. So take that Double Decker tourist bus and find out all sorts of crazy things about your city that you had no idea were even true stories. This date is really a cute one, and it gives you an excuse to do all the looking up at tall buildings that you were too embarrassed to do walking around as a native.

15. Take a class.

Woodworking, yoga or PowerPoint, perhaps? It doesn't matter what the class is, but if it's a one-day course and it engages various people all at once, it could be fun. What sounds more exhilarating than discussing what your parents do for work over the sound of power tools? If, by some kismet chance, you both realized that you really loved graphic design, but know little to nothing about it, it could be great to grab a continuing education course at some nearby community college and get to know it together! This date is another win-win, since no matter how you end up feeling about the date, you've earned a valuable skill and cultivated a new hobby.

16. Agree to a picnic.

This one may be the most typical out of the bunch, but you can still make it pretty interesting. Don't just buy all of the snacks and foods for your picnic premade. Make it into a potluck, and try making as much as you can on your own, to share with the other person. This personal investment will make the reward that much sweeter and you'll both appreciate the massive effort invested. Be sure to weed out any dietary restrictions or allergies that your date may have, however, so you avoid having your first date in the ER. And don't worry, that location didn't make this list.

17. <u>Grab a park bench and never leave.</u>

Though this is similar to the public transportation date, it affords you more to look at and the beauty of fresh air from the outside world. You'll get to do lots of people watching, and this isn't necessarily a strictly warm weather date, although cold weather may keep it from being a "never leave" date. Watching the scenery change around in front of you can be pretty interesting, especially if you're stationed in a particularly active park, like one smack dab in the middle of your town. Chances are you'll miss a little of the outside world anyway, at least if you're engrossed in your date. But just in case you aren't, there will be lots else to see instead.

18. <u>Let someone else choose!</u>

If neither of you can decide on a date of your own, have one of your friends do it for you! It's totally okay to be somewhat baffled, and leave it to a wildcard draw. Of course, you can always veto the decision or have them draft up a list of different places they think might work that you can then choose from. It can be a friend of yours, or a friend of your date's, but either way, it keeps it interesting. Especially if you have the kind of situation where even though you've just started dating, you and your date are notorious for heading to the same places over and over. Plus, you know the old saying: three heads are better than two!

19. <u>Meet up *before* work.</u>

Stay with me, here, friends...this is definitely quirky. But it could be so much fun! You could meet up before work, decide if you're interested in one another and then even call in sick or just show up late! I haven't tried it out yet, but it seems like it could be really cool with another super open-minded person. I'm also not the biggest early bird (definitely more of a night owl) but I love the serenity and quiet that the early morning affords us. It's a great time to get privacy, while everyone else is sitting in his or her office. If you also work in an office, when else will you get so much time away from so many people?

20. <u>Google a word and your city and let your imaginations run wild.</u>

What if you just typed in "Monster" and "Minnesota" to your Google search engine and saw what came up? What if it was the largest toy store in the state and it was a legitimately doable traveling distance? Would you be willing to go check it out with a date? If both of you are good natured and adventurous people (I know quite a few of those) it could be a great and hilarious time for both of you. And who knows, maybe one of you will come out of it with a new gaming device for a niece or nephew.

Chapter 8: Reading Your Man: How To Know When It's a Go!

More than a few times, I've been perplexed by the actions of a man I was dating. He didn't text often enough—was he really interested? Or he text messaged ultra-fast and ultra-often? Super desperate? Being the super-investigator that I am, I was left wondering at every waking moment and examining the smallest of things to see if a guy was a dud or the real deal.

Is it love at first sight? Or maybe even lust? At the beginning of a new relationship it can be difficult to know which sentiment, if either, are permeating your man's mind. Instead of scrutinizing every single statement or action or even text message, focus on the facts at hand and the interactions in the present.

SEE WHAT HE HAS TO <u>SAY.</u>

Remember what I'd mentioned before about securing a second date using a mutually desirable activity? In the same way that you can suggest that the two of you do something together again, one of the easiest ways to gauge his interest is if he invites you to another event during the first date.

DON'T GO CRAZY OVERANALYZING VOICEMAILS AND TEXT MESSAGES.

If I had a nickel for every time a friend asked me to help decipher online messages, or text message and voicemails, I'd be rich enough to buy my dream guy. If I also received a nickel for every time I did it, I could probably buy two. I am among the most over-analytical people I know and it shows. That is how I taught myself to take it down a couple notches, take a deep breath and reevaluate why I was sweating the little things so much and so often.

a. Guys aren't reading anywhere *near* as deeply into what they've sent.
b. The kinds of things that people send in brief messages don't always correctly or thoroughly convey whatever thought they had in mind.

MAKE SURE YOU'RE NOT JUST ANOTHER GIRL.

You know, sometimes it's okay to be just another girl to a guy that you are dating. Maybe he is just another guy to you as well. You're casually dating and nothing has been set in mutual exclusivity. But sometimes, that is not the case and you desire more out of your interactions with this person. Now, you have to consider a couple of things and learn whether or not you actually stand out in his dating scene.

a. <u>How often do you see one another?</u>

If you only see this guy once or twice a week, depending on how busy your schedules are, it's very possible that he's hanging out with another lady. But before you get all bent out of shape over it, consider the fact that you're probably not exclusive yet. If you're seeing one another more often than not, and that includes a fair amount of sleepovers, I think it's safe to say that you're the main woman on his agenda. And for now, until exclusivity happens, I would say being the main woman on his agenda is exactly where you want to be right now. Don't push for too much too soon, or you might make him feel anxious about how fast everything is moving.

b. <u>Does he often remember what you tell him?</u>

A surefire sign of a really cool guy that's totally into you is if he's thoughtful enough to remember a few important things about your likes and dislikes, or some story you've told him and the subtle hints you drop. First off, a guy who remembers these things actually cared enough to listen. Great strategy. Secondly, the more he remembers, the less likely he has had to remember information about other women, or—and this is definitely the best-case scenario—the less he probably cared about retaining the other women's information. This is great for you.

READ BODY LANGUAGE!

Hopefully by now, you have touched him, both emotionally and *physically*. So, when he is with you, is he engaged? If he does the following, you're in a great place.

- <u>Sits facing you directly and makes direct eye contact when he talks?</u>

  This is a great sign. Also useful is when he leans into you during a discussion. This totally shows not only an interest in you but his really trying to grasp and identify with what you're saying. If he raises his eyebrows, but not as though he's shocked, that is his way of taking in as much as his eyes will allow. You're a brand new person that he's just met, and you've obviously piqued his interest and/or impressed him.

- o Can't stop smiling or even smirking.

  This is a great scenario! And pretty straightforward. But it's important to note that it has to be directly at *you*, of course.

- o <u>Reaches out to touch you, or your hair, etc?</u> He's looking for an excuse to get close to you, but the great thing about the hair touching is that it's way more intimate and may hint at the fact that he's not just looking solely for sex.
- o <u>Finger combing his hair?</u> Then your man is likely *preening*— you know, just like birds do to attract potential mates. If he's smiling at you and running his hands through his hair, it's a subconscious means of making sure he looks good in the moment and attracts attention to himself, and it looks good for you! It is especially evident if it happens when you're approaching him or he is approaching you.

- Talking with his hands? The more a man gesticulates, the more he probably likes you. Talking with your hands illustrates a good communicator, but it can also mean he is trying with more effort to get the words out, since using your hands helps you express information more smoothly. If his hand is outstretched, even better, since it translates into a request for bodily contact. If you notice that his hand is extended far across the table, towards your side, he is sending definite signs.
- Check out his posturing. If he's standing erect (hey now, take your mind out of the gutter) with his chest out and in a flattering position of sitting up straight, he is trying to make his body look its best.
- Have these things occurred *after* you've already slept together?

It may sound crass but we all know that many people (notoriously, but not necessarily exclusive to men!) are out to go on tons of dates for only one reason: to get laid. Some of the worst offenders won't even return a phone call or a text message after they've slept with you once. They've gotten what they wanted and now they're essentially done with you.

It's not necessarily always malicious (read: casual vs. romantic relationships), but you'll need to know how to assess. All asshole moves aside, if a gentleman is still very into you after he's already gotten what you both wanted, it is a fantastic sign. It shows that you've gotten beyond arguably the most exciting step in the dating pyramid and there's still an interest in spending time together.

IS HIS PROFILE STILL UP?

This is pretty self explanatory. If your potential love match still has his profile up on the website through which you two met, it speaks volumes.

- Check his last login.

Don't be sketchy about it, but if you can find a way to check out his last login without making it awkward—as in his knowing that you've visited his page *post dating involvement*—you may be able to enlighten yourself as to his status. A great way to do this without jumping through hoops and being too involved is if you have a good friend who also utilizes the same online dating site. They can look into when the guy you're really interested last logged in.

Even a friend of a friend will do (and perhaps it may be better, in the event that your close friend's involvement can be traced back to you)! However, no matter what, don't your DARE create a new, dummy profile and use it to snoop. That is when things get borderline creepy, because unless you two have sworn to exclusivity, he doesn't owe you anything in terms of taking down his profile.

- Is he constantly checking his phone whenever you're together?

  You aren't allowed to do it, so he's not allowed to break the rules either. If he's constantly on his phone when you guys are out, it could be a bad sign that he's either indifferent or may be messaging other ladies.

Still a little bit confused, huh? How about this:

IT'S LOOKING PRETTY GOOD IF:

- <u>He calls or messages you early on in the day!</u>

  It shows that he's hopeful, and is leaving enough time for you to make plans later on, if need be. Obviously, you don't want to be involved with the guy who only messages you after dark, looking for a hook up (unless that is something you've pre-established). Or the guy who messages you long after the work day, looking to make plans to go out because his other plans fell through.

- He really wants to meet your friends?

    Awesome! Any guy who wants to genuinely get to know your friends intends to be around for a while, or at the very least is good-natured. See how he interacts with them, because it will make a world of difference. Everyone knows that you can't have a successful relationship with someone if they don't get along with your friends. If he asks them interesting questions and feels comfortable making jokes with them, that's a great start. Ensure that he's not trying too hard, and definitely make sure that he isn't deciding which one of them he'd date first if you two ever stopped dating.

- He's interested in meeting for a coffee.

    Wow! You're both going to be sober? This is *huge*. As I've mentioned before and as we all know, it's definitely telling if someone is only willing to meet up with you after 9 or 10pm: that is thinly veiled, late night casual encounter business that's going to go on. So when a guy is interested in seeing you in the daytime for lunch or something similar, and the intention to hang out until the wee hours of the night is highly unlikely, it's a great sign! It means he's actually interested in getting to know you, and not just getting inside of your pants. Congratulations.

- He keeps in contact during his work hours.

    Maybe you're adding some much needed sunlight to his otherwise dreary work schedule. Either way, distracting himself by contacting you specifically, be it through email or text message means you're on his mind.

IT'S NOT LOOKING GOOD IF:

- You never hang out completely alone.

He invited you to hang out! Yay! Then you arrive and he's with his lesbian friend, Diana. Boo. A guy who is really and truly interested in you will want to spend quality alone time with you. He will want to have you all to himself at least *some* of the time, especially since enough quality alone time will likely pave the way for sexual encounters to come. Additionally, he may be well aware of how you feel about him. Inviting you out, but only when he's with his friends, may be a tool that he's using to avoid having the awkward conversation with you about how you feel about him. Sneaky, sneaky.

- <u>He takes forever to respond to your messages.</u>

Voicemail, email or text message, you don't hear back from him until the dead of night. Admit it: he's probably been busy pining after some other girl, or just busy not being busy with you. When you meet someone new, guy or girl, your instinct is to be excited when you hear from him or her. The chance to hang out with that person or keep in contact is interesting and it's also something you genuinely crave. If he can't be bothered to message you back in a timely fashion, he probably doesn't want to be bothered.

- <u>He's willing to divulge information about his escapades with other women.</u>

Any guy who is willing to do this really doesn't even see you as a competitor in the competition for his affection. Guy or girl, no one is silly enough to blurt out what they're up to with other members of the opposite sex. It makes you feel as though you're just a number. If all heterosexual women of the world know one thing, it's that we crave that feeling of distinction from all other females; we love the illusion that a guy creates when we feel as if we're the only girl in the world he has eyes for.

A man who asks you for advice on whether or not another woman is interested in him, is not interested in you. Sorry. I would suggest you make it a point to chuck him into the "friend zone" and quit trying to convince him of otherwise.

Even though it hasn't been said outright, he's made it pretty clear that he's not into you in that romantic kind of way. And if this is some sort of cheap trick he's employing to garner your attention and possible jealousy? Run for the hills, because this guy is a player, or worse.

- The plans that he makes with you are too casual.

  Texting you "Drinks later?" At 6pm on the day-of may seem spontaneous and exciting, but it may very well mean that he had other plans that didn't make it through, or didn't manage to lock down any at all with a girl he's really interested in. Don't become a victim of this fair weather dating type. If you let him get away with it once, it will become a really annoying habit.

o He doesn't offer to foot the bill. At all. Ever.

  Even the most feminist of men will enjoy the comfort and companionship of being with an awesome woman. If he ALWAYS expects you to pay for lunches, dinners, getaways, even something as silly as condoms? This guy is a good for nothing and even if he thinks he's being fair by leveling the playing field and allowing a woman to take charge, he doesn't sound even remotely fair. (Disclaimer: purchasing of condoms is silly in terms of its relatively inconsequential monetary value, NOT IN TERMS OF ITS POTENTIAL TO PROTECT AGAINST SEXUALLY TRANSMITTED DISEASES AND PREGNANCY. Glad we've cleared that up.)

Chapter 9: The Dominance and the Detriment: Online Dating, Tales of Success and Disaster

What kind of guide would this be without a couple of great anecdotes detailing both the amazing and horrific true accounts of ladies in dating? Not the one I've set here before you! So I list here for your perusal, a couple of stories that are sure to bring a scoff, or a smile to your face ☺ (Names have been changed to protect the innocent.)

MY FIRST ONLINE DATE was completely unintentional. At some point during my junior year of college, a friend and I wound up on some website to take a quiz and ended up being forced to sign up for said site. Once we realized there was online dating involved as well, we thought it'd be a lark to fill out our profiles and peek at others. After a while, we'd completely forgotten about it. That is, until I got an email from the site letting me know that someone had viewed my profile. After curiously checking this guy out, his profile seemed interesting and best of all, there was a picture of him in a suit. How could it go wrong?

In so many ways. The first time we met up, was with my friends— my first mistake! He was dressed in a suit and tie, but not just any suit and tie. Completely formal, almost comical and definitely not something that you would just wear casually to your office job. He was a completely awkward, 6'2 22-year-old who had the appearance of a large bird but wanted to become a bodybuilder. And he lived at home with his mother. I dated him for a solid three months, probably out of pity but mostly boredom. Aren't you glad I decided to share?

"WHERE'S MY WALLET?" was what my girlfriend Becca heard, as the guy she was seeing scoured his pockets, looking for his debit card. The bill for their drinks had totaled $56.92, and it looked like Becca was going to be taking care of it whether she wanted to or not. Besides having been incredibly boring and also looking way, way older than his pictures made him seem, her date had practically invited himself to her coworker's birthday party. Even though she had strategically placed the time of the date to not counter her full-on nighttime plans. Once there, everyone was convinced that he was her boyfriend, to her great dismay. After the extended-date was over, he texted her to let her know he had a *great* time, and that if she wanted to he was more than willing to meet up again and take care of drinks. Needless to say, she wasn't interested.

If you think these are bad…well, I'll leave you with an awesome one.

AMAZING ARCHITECTURE was all that Kelly could see after her date with a 40-year-old architect from New Zealand. Having been 22 at the time, she knew it was a stretch and that a lot people would have a lot of things to say about the age difference. But so what? It was just one date and she had taken her dating efforts online so that she could get to know all kinds of different people and broaden her datingsphere. She had been so intrigued by the thorough and enticing back and forth banter they had shared in the messages over their online dating site. So the next thing Kelly knew, she was headed to a wine bar is a very, very hip part of town.

Initially completely worried that her date's age would immediately show and that the pictures on his profile were likely to be more flattering than they should have, she felt a rush of relief when she arrived at the bar and saw him smiling at her, looking pretty decent. Although it was obvious that he was older, he was good-natured and had youthfulness about him, and she could swear that she caught a trace of his accent from what must have been his time in New Zealand possibly decades ago.

And again, before she knew it, he was telling her all sorts of incredible stories about the work that he did, and he was amused by her dry sense of humor. One hour turned into three and one glass of wine turned into three and they needed to grab something to eat. As they headed to their next location, it began to rain and slowly but surely the drops got heavier. They made a run for it, and ended up near the park. By this time, it was nearing midnight and maybe the witching hour got the best of them, because he took her hand, guided her over to a large tree and planted an awesome kiss on her.

We're not children here; we know what happened next. After a few minutes of super intense kissing, they headed back towards his apartment. Two fully consenting adults had decided to get sexual on the first date! Who'd have thought, huh? Anyway, I won't get into the sordid details, but they slept together and she had an amazing time. His apartment and career were impressive, and more importantly , *he* was impressive. He desperately wanted Kelly to stay, but she actually had friends to meet after their encounter. Can you believe that?! Only a 22-year old...

So there you have it! You take the good, you take the bad and everything hilarious and awesome in between.

Chapter 10: Go Forth...AND FLIRT!

Online dating may seem easy enough—and don't get me wrong, it can be—but it can also be pretty easily mishandled. If you utilize all of my advice to the best of your ability, you are sure to steer clear of easily avoidable and super common dating mistakes. The more often you participate in browsing profiles, sending messages and meeting up for real-life dates, the faster you'll be an old pro at it. For so many people, dating and self-confidence go hand in hand. Becoming romantically involved with someone means you consider yourself to be valuable to another person, and that can be a difficult conceit for some individuals. With a little patience and a lot of practice, online dating will allow your self-confidence will grow by leaps and bounds.

Another important fact to leave fresh in your mind is your how strengthening your confidence will affect your feelings of safety and capability in terms of meeting strangers. As heterosexual women, we sometimes have it much more difficult than men when it comes to feeling safe and sound in a dating environment, let alone one with a system that begin almost anonymously and primarily online. Even in this day and age, we have to be extremely careful of who we allow into our lives, our social circles, and our homes as well as our hearts. So bear that in mind if you ever get the sneaking suspicion that you are unhappy with a potential mate.

It takes one savvy lady to accept the responsibility of keeping herself safe and happy while also being adventurous and putting herself out there, open to the possibility of love, happiness and the occasional hook up. Remember the notations in this guide on following your instincts, not feeling intimidated and generally keeping your wits about you at all times.

Finally, don't get discouraged with your online dating venture simply because your first date was a total bust, for instance. Where would I be if I had done that? Definitely not the author of How-To Do Online Dating for Women. Consider this: if you went on a date with a guy you met through a friend, or in a bar, and it ended up being completely terrible, your first reaction wouldn't be to immediately stop dating forever, would it? So why should dating online be any different? It's only a new venue for meeting a bunch of eligible, willing singles who are all taking the same leap of faith that you are.

So once again, stay happy, healthy, engaged in your online dating experiences and the development of your amazing and exciting new love life!

About Expert

Amma Ampofo has written avidly since she was first able to hold a pen, transforming into her mastery of the word processing machine. Somewhere around that time, she developed an immense and honest interest in the opposite sex.

Since then, she's been navigating the big, bad world of dating and transformed herself from a clueless lady to a sage man-eater.

Though she may fall into the category of what most consider a late bloomer, Amma has more than made up for lost time in the sheer volume of her dating (mis)adventures, ranging from awful to awesome and every single adjective in between.

One of her favorite pastimes involves fielding questions from friends regarding their love lives, and the preponderance of sex and relationships in general. But if Amma has any one bit of die-hard advice to offer in terms of getting what you want out of love, it all comes right back to never settling for what you don't want, and knowing what you're worth.

HowExpert publishes quick 'how to' guides on all topics from A to Z by everyday experts. Visit HowExpert.com to learn more.

Recommended Resources

- HowExpert.com – Quick 'How To' Guides on All Topics from A to Z by Everyday Experts.
- HowExpert.com/free – Free HowExpert Email Newsletter.
- HowExpert.com/books – HowExpert Books
- HowExpert.com/courses – HowExpert Courses
- HowExpert.com/clothing – HowExpert Clothing
- HowExpert.com/membership – HowExpert Membership Site
- HowExpert.com/affiliates – HowExpert Affiliate Program
- HowExpert.com/writers – Write About Your #1 Passion/Knowledge/Expertise & Become a HowExpert Author.
- HowExpert.com/resources – Additional HowExpert Recommended Resources
- YouTube.com/HowExpert – Subscribe to HowExpert YouTube.
- Instagram.com/HowExpert – Follow HowExpert on Instagram.
- Facebook.com/HowExpert – Follow HowExpert on Facebook.